I0016012

JAVA Programming

Intermediate Concepts For the Fundamentals
of Object Oriented Programming

Table of Contents

INTRODUCTION

Congratulations on downloading JAVA Programming: Intermediate Concepts For the Fundamentals of Object Oriented Programming, and thank you for doing so!

The following chapters will discuss the intermediate tools of JAVA programming, its uses, and how to write JAVA code for yourself. This book is a continuation of the book JAVA Programming: An Introduction, History, and the Fundamentals for Creating Your First Program, and should be used in conjunction with it for maximum effect. The content is written under the assumption that the reader has at least a beginner level understanding of Java code and syntax.

There are plenty of books on this subject available on the market, so thank you again for choosing this JAVA Programming series! Every effort was made to ensure this book is full of as much useful information as possible. Please enjoy!

CHAPTER 1

CONTROL FLOW, AND
HOW TO USE IT

Control Flow

Computer Science defines control flow, or flow control as the sequence where particular statements, function calls, and instructions are evaluated or executed
from a programming paradigm that alters a program's
state. The explicit control flows highlights and signifies
the difference between a declarative programming from
an imperative programming language.

Inside an imperative programming language, a flow
control statement executes products referred to follow
between two or more paths. A group of stand-alone elements is widely designed as a block, defining a lexical
scope. While signals, and interrupts are a low-level
mechanism that can change the flow control, in contrast
to a subroutine. For the responses to outside stimulus,
compared to the execution of in-line flow control statement the latter may occur asynchronously.

Lastly, flow control instructions at the level of assem-
bly language commonly work by modifying the program
counter. The Central processing units (CPUs) for some

control flow instruction are only available on uncondi-tional or conditional jumps, also known as branch in-structions.

Categories of control flow statements

> Jump
> Conditional branch
> Subroutines
> Coroutines
> Continuation
> Unconditional Halt

Continuation in a different statement is known as an unconditional branch. The initializing of a group of standalone elements for a few present conditions, as well as the repeated execution of a set of statements, are known as a conditional branch. While the start-up of dis-tant statements preceding the flow control customarily returns continuations, subroutines, and coroutines. And stopping the program, to prevent future executions is called an unconditional halt. These are the functions of the categories of control flow statements.

Java control flow statements

The standalone elements manipulate the order of in-itialization in a java program, coming from data values and logic. Java has three general categories of flow con-trol statements.

Selection statements

> The if, if-else and switch.
> Loop statements
> The while, do-while and for.
> Transfer statements

- ➢ The break, continue, return, try-catch-finally and assert.
- ➢ Control statements are used when the user wants to modify the embedded sequential order of execution.

The if-then Statement

The **if-then statement** is a control flow type of statement. It is also considered the most basic in its class. This statement commands the program to start-up a certain area of code when some conditions are met. This happens when a certain logical test returns true instead of false.

Example:

```
void stopvehicle() {
    // logical test to see if Myvehicle class is moving
    if (isrolling){
        // the "then" clause will reduce vehicle Speed
        vehicleSpeed--;
    }
}
```

In this sample code, the Myvehicle class can allow the brakes to decrease the tricycle's speed only if the tricycle started rolling.

Must the test produces a "false" denoting a halt of movement from the tricycle. The manipulation jumps to the end of the if-then unequaled statement. If the "then" clause only has one statement, then the closing and opening braces will just become optional.

```
void stopvehicle() {
    if (isrolling) {
```

```
      vehicleSpeed--;
   } else {
      System.err.println("The vehicle has stopped.");
   }
}
```

Another example:

```
class IfElseDemo {
    public static void main(String[] args) {

        int testscore = 76;
        char grade;

        if (testscore >= 90) {
            grade = 'A';
        } else if (testscore >= 80) {
            grade = 'B';
        } else if (testscore >= 70) {
            grade = 'C';
        } else if (testscore >= 60) {
            grade = 'D';
        } else {
            grade = 'F';
        }
        System.out.println("Grade = " + grade);
    }
}
```

The final product from the code provided above shows us that Grade = C

The user may infer that the value or data variable *testscore* can be related to more one and in some cases more expressions. In this example it relates to several expressions, given the 76 >= 60 and 76 >= 70 compound statement. When the prerequisites are satisfied, the needed statements are initialized (grade = 'C';), then the remaining conditions will not be evaluated.

Switch Statement

The switch statement can have some of the possible execution paths. A switch works with the char, short, byte, and int primitive data types. In addition, the switch also works with enumerated types represented in Enum Types. A number of special classes that cover specific primitive types Integer, Short, Byte, and Character explained in strings and numbers.

```
int month = 8;
if (month == 1) {
    System.out.println("January");
} else if (month == 2) {
    System.out.println("February");
}
...  // and so on
```

The example above shows that August is printed as the final output.

A switch block is the body of a switch statement named with a single or more default labels. This type of statement evaluates its own expression and executes all elements that precede the identical case label. This could also be displayed using the if-then-else statements. See example below,

```
public class SwitchDemo {
    public static void main(String[] args) {

        int month = 8;
        String monthString;
        switch (month) {
            case 1:  monthString = "January";
                     break;
            case 2:  monthString = "February";
                     break;
            case 3:  monthString = "March";
                     break;
            case 4:  monthString = "April";
                     break;
            case 5:  monthString = "May";
                     break;
            case 6:  monthString = "June";
                     break;

            case 7:  monthString = "July";
                     break;
            case 8:  monthString = "August";
                     break;
            case 9:  monthString = "September";
                     break;
            case 10: monthString = "October";
                     break;
            case 11: monthString = "November";
                     break;
            case 12: monthString = "December";
                     break;
            default: monthString = "Invalid month";
                     break;
        }
        System.out.println(monthString);
    }
}
```

Choosing between the switch statement or the if-then-else statement for use on execution should be based on the expressions and the readability that the statement is examining. The if-then-else statements are meant for expressions based on areas of conditions or values, while the switch statement is tried for expressions based on single integers, string object, or enumerated value.

In Java version, SE 7 and later, the user can use expressions from the switch statement. The below example presents the month from the amount of the string named month.

```java
public class StringSwitchDemo {

    public static int getMonthNumber(String month) {

        int monthNumber = 0;

        if (month == null) {
            return monthNumber;
        }

        switch (month.toLowerCase()) {
            case "january":
                monthNumber = 1;
                break;
            case "february":
                monthNumber = 2;
                break;
            case "march":
                monthNumber = 3;
                break;
            case "april":
                monthNumber = 4;
                break;
```

```
case "may":
    monthNumber = 5;
    break;
case "june":
    monthNumber = 6;
    break;
case "july":
    monthNumber = 7;
    break;
case "august":
    monthNumber = 8;
    break;
case "september":
    monthNumber = 9;
    break;
case "october":
    monthNumber = 10;
    break;
case "november":
    monthNumber = 11;
    break;
```

```
                    case "december":
                        monthNumber = 12;
                        break;
                    default:
                        monthNumber = 0;
                        break;
            }

            return monthNumber;
        }

        public static void main(String[] args) {

            String month = "August";

            int returnedMonthNumber =

    StringSwitchDemo.getMonthNumber(month);

            if (returnedMonthNumber == 0) {
                System.out.println("Invalid month");
            } else {


    System.out.println(returnedMonthNumber);
                }
            }
        }
```

The final output is 8.

The expressions are correlated with each case label. The StringSwitchDemo example should permit any month disregarding any type of case. The month is changed to lowercase using the toLowerCase approach and all other strings identified with case labels are all in the same format.

The example confirms the expression found in the switch statement as a null. Users must ensure that the expression in any of this statement is not null to avoid NullPointerException from being launched.

CHAPTER 2

HOW TO USE WHILE, DO-WHILE, AND FOR STATEMENTS

The while statement continuously initiates a block of statements when a certain status is true. Expressing a syntax such as below:

```
while (expression) {
    statement(s)
}
```

The while statement calculates expression, which should return a boolean value. If the expression evaluates to true, the while statement initiates the statement(s) in the while block. The statement will continue its testing of the expression and execute its block until the expression would appraise to false. Using the while statement to print the values from 1 through 10 can be done as in the example WhileDemo program:

```
class WhileDemo {
    public static void main(String[] args){
        int count = 1;
        while (count < 11) {
            System.out.println("Count is: " + count);
            count++;
```

```
        }
    }
}
```

You can manifest an infinite loop with the use of the while statement as follows:

```
while (true){
    // your code goes here
}
```

The Java programming language can provide a do-while statement. That can be performed as follows:

```
do {
    statement(s)
} while (expression);
```

The difference between do-while conditional looping statement and while loop statement is that do-while statement makes a logical evaluation of the accompanying expression at the very end. On the other hand, the while statement evaluates the included expression in the syntax at the start of the loop.

In conclusion, the statements that are found inside the do { } section of the code will usually be executed at least one time. That concept is illustrated in the following DoWhileDemo code below:

```
class DoWhileDemo {
    public static void main(String[] args){
        int count = 1;
        do {
            System.out.println("Count is: " + count);
            count++;
        } while (count < 11);
    }
}
```

Summary

The statements mentioned above are the most basic of all the flow control statements. The if-then communicate with your program, in order to execute some region of code if a certain test evaluates to true. The if-then-else statement gives another choice of path for execution during an "if" clause classifies to false. Compared to the if-then-else and if-then where execution is only limited to a certain number of paths. The switch statement grants for zero or more than one available execution paths. The do-while statements continuously initiate a block of statements when a certain status is true, evaluating its expression in the foundation of the loop. The statements inside the do block are often executed on at least a minimum count of one. The for standalone element gives the user an intact path to repeat or reintroduce among a range of values. The for statement has two forms which were structured for looping pass arrays and collections.

CHAPTER 3

NESTED LOOPS

A nested loop is a loop that is within the parameters of another loop. Below is an example of a nested loop:

```
for (int i = 1; i <= 5; ++i) {

    // codes inside the body of outer loop

    for (int j = 1; j <=2; ++j) {
        // codes inside the body of both outer and inner
loop
    }

    // codes inside the body of outer loop}
```

The a for loop is within the frame of the other for loop.

Example 1:

```
class NestedForLoop {
    public static void main(String[] args) {

        for (int i = 1; i <= 5; ++i) {

            System.out.println("Outer loop iteration " + i);

            for (int j = 1; j <=2; ++j) {
                System.out.println("i = " + i + "; j = " + j);
            }
        }
    }}
```

14

When the user runs the program it will give an output as presented below:

Outer loop iteration 1
$i = 1; j = 1$
$i = 1; j = 2$
Outer loop iteration 2
$i = 2; j = 1$
$i = 2; j = 2$
Outer loop iteration 3
$i = 3; j = 1$
$i = 3; j = 2$
Outer loop iteration 4
$i = 4; j = 1$
$i = 4; j = 2$
Outer loop iteration 5
$i = 5; j = 1$
$i = 5; j = 2$

As you can see in this code, the iteration called outer loop is reintroduced 5 times. The inner loop, on the other hand, is executed over 2 times each time outer loop is executed.

Here's an example:

```
class NestedLoop {
  public static void main(String[] args) {

    int i = 1;

    while (i <= 5) {

      System.out.println("Outer loop iteration " + i);

      for (int j = 1; j <= 2; ++j) {
        System.out.println("i = " + i + "; j = " + j);
      }

      ++i;
    }
  }}
```

The product of this program shows that the outer loop repeats five times. In each repetition of the outer loop, the inner loop iterates for two times.

Outer loop iteration 1
i = 1; j = 1
i = 1; j = 2
Outer loop iteration 2
i = 2; j = 1
i = 2; j = 2
Outer loop iteration 3
i = 3; j = 1
i = 3; j = 2
Outer loop iteration 4
i = 4; j = 1
i = 4; j = 2
Outer loop iteration 5
i = 5; j = 1
i = 5; j = 2

Creating a pattern using nested loops.

```
1
1 2
1 2 3
1 2 3 4
1 2 3 4 5
```

The user can use the below program to create the above pattern.

```java
class Pattern {
    public static void main(String[] args) {

        int rows = 5;

        for(int i = 1; i <= rows; ++i)
        {
            for(int j = 1; j <= i; ++j)
            {
                System.out.print(j + " ");
            }
            System.out.println("");
        }
    }}
```

Another example:

```
        1
      1 2
    1 2 3
  1 2 3 4 5
    1 2 3
      1 2
        1
```

The programmer can create the above pattern with the use of the program below:

```java
public class NewFile{

  public static void main(String []args){
    int k = 0;
    for (int i=1 ; i<=5 ; i++)
      {
      { for (int h=2 ; h >= i ; h--)
           System.out.print(" ");
       for (int j=1 ; j<= i + k ; j++)
         System.out.print(j);
       for (int w=2 ; w>= i; w--)
         System.out.print(" ");

         }
         k++;
         System.out.println();}
  }}
```

Yielding this output:

```
    1
   123
  12345
 1234567
123456789
```

The user must divide the code into an upper and lower triangle using two loops. The integer "n" for the figure below signifies the tallness of the diamond in characters.

```java
int i = 0, j, k, n;
 n = 7; // 7 characters high. Change as needed.

 for (k = 1; k <= (n + 1) / 2; k++) {
    for (i = 0; i < n - k; i++) {
        System.out.print(" ");
    }
    for (j = 0; j < k; j++) {
        System.out.print("* ");
    }
    System.out.println("");
}

 for (k = ((n + 1) / 2); k < n; k++) {
    for (i = 1; i < k; i++) {
        System.out.print(" ");
    }
    for (j = 0; j < n - k; j++) {
        System.out.print(" *");
    }
    System.out.println("");
}
```

Complex Output

In writing a nested for loop in order to produce a certain output, the user should build multiple complex lines. Using an external vertical loop for individual lines and the internal horizontal loop for the patterns inside each line.

The outer and inner loop

The first step is to write the outer loop, from one towards the number lines.

```
for (int line = 1; line <= 5; line++) {

...

}
```

Each line has an arrangement. Zero dots followed by a number.

```
. . . .1
. . .2
. .3
.4
5
```

The quantity of the dots is relevant to the line number.

Scalings loops to numbers

```
for (int count = 1; count <= 5; count++) {

System.out.print( ... );

}
```

The printed output would be,

```
4 7 10 13 16
for (int count = 1; count <= 5; count++) { System.out.print(3 * count + 1 + " ");
}
```

Loop Tables

In order to see scales or patterns, construct a table of count and the numbers. For a statement to print an output like below.

2 7 12 17 22

Whenever the count would increase by one, the number should go up by five. However count * 5 is higher by three, so we subtract three.

count	number to print	5 * count	5 * count - 3
1	2	5	2
2	7	10	7
3	12	15	12
4	17	20	17
5	22	25	22

Slope Intercept

Slope Intercept is the mathematical basis for the loop tables.

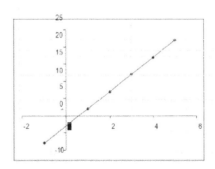

count (x)	number to print (y)
1	2
2	7
3	12
4	17
5	22

The user should recall the slope-intercept form and its formula y = mx + b.

The slope is known as "rise over run" (e.g. rise / run). Considering that the "run" is always one the user must raise along x by one, the user must need to view at the "rise." The rise represents the difference of the different y values. You can call the slope as the slope (m). In the current sample, the value is positive five (+5).

You can use the following lines to compute for the needed values:

y = mx + b
2 = (5)(1) + b
b = -3

Therefore,
y = mx + b
Y = 5x - 3
Y = (5)(count) - 3

count (x)	number to print (y)
1	2
2	7
3	12
4	17
5	22

Algebraically, anyone always takes the value of y at x equaling to one, and then you can solve for the value of the variable b as follows:

$y = mx + b$
$y1 = m(1) + b$
$y1 = m + b$
$b = y1 - m$

Specifically, subtracting the slope from the first y value:

$b = 2 - 5 = -3$

This will give you the value for the y-intercept. You will then arrive at the equation below:

$y = mx + b$
$y = 5x - 3$
$y = (5)(count) - 3$

CHAPTER 4

BREAK STATEMENTS

The break statement has two isolated and particular uses: leaving a loop and leaving a switch statement. You can't utilize a break at any place just inside a switch statement or a loop. Below is the syntax of a break statement:

```
break;
```

Leaving a loop

Inside any sort of a loop, break makes the loop exit. There is only a small reason for having a bare break that categorically leaves a loop. Quite often, the break is inserted in a statement. See below example:

```
for (int i = 0; i < myArray.length; i++) {
    if (myArray[i] < 0) {
        System.out.println("Bad value in location " + i);
        break;
    }
}
```

On account of nested loops, break leaves the deepest circle. Utilization of the break statement is often disheartened. Because, this is on account if it enables the user to leave the loop in more than one way; the typical exit, in addition to any conditions that cause a break, which can be complicated. It implies that you may need to compose an extra code, after the loop, to give light of what the loop did. Subsequently, before you break out of a loop, you ought to attempt to discover another approach to get similar outcomes.

Exiting

The switch statement gives you a chance to pick which of a few blocks of code to execute. Unless you put a break after each block of code, execution streams into the following block. See below example:

```java
switch (grade) {
    case 'A':
        System.out.println("You did great!");
        break;
    case 'B':
    case 'C':
    case 'D':
        System.out.println("You passed.");
    case 'F':
        System.out.println("You flunked!");
}
```

Based on the above code:

If grade is equal to 'A', Java prints "You did great!" and the switch statement exits.

If grade is equal to 'F', Java prints "You flunked!" and the switch statement exits.

If grade is equal to 'B', 'C', or 'D', Java prints "You passed.", because the 'B' case flows into the 'C' case, which flows into the 'D' case. However, in these three cases it also prints "You flunked!", because there is no break to prevent the 'D' case from flowing into the 'F' case.

The necessity for break articulations inside a switch statement is generally viewed as a poor language plan, yet it is reliable with C and numerous other more established programming languages. Another way of exiting from multiple levels of switch statements or loops is through the use of labels which will be tackled on the succeeding topics.

Applying break statements inside loops

The break statement enables you to leave a loop from any point inside its body, bypassing its typical end expression. At the point when the break statement is experienced inside a loop, the loop is quickly ended, and program control resumes at the following statement taking after the loop. The break statement can be utilized with each of the three of C's loops. You can have the same number of statements inside a loop as you yearn. It is usually best to utilize the break for unique purposes, not as your ordinary loop exit. break is likewise utilized as a part of conjunction with capacities and case statements.

The continue statement is to some degree the inverse of the break statement. It drives the following emphasis of the loop to occur, avoiding any code in the middle of itself and the test state of the loop. In while and do-while loops, a continue statement will make control go specifically to the test condition and after that proceed with the looping procedure. On account of the for loop, the augmentation of some portion of the loop continues. One great utilization of continue is to restart a statement succession when a mistake happens.

```
#include $$$$stdio.h&&&&

main( )

{

int x ;

for ( x=0 ; x$$$$=100 ; x++) {

if (x%2) continue;

printf("%d\n" , x);

}

}
```

Yielding a remainder of a over b, and 0 when there is no remainder present.

Below is an example of the utilization for the break statement:

```
#include $$$$stdio.h&&&&

main( )

{

int t ;

for ( ; ; ) {

scanf("%d" , &t) ;

if ( t==10 ) break ;

}

printf("End of an infinite loop...\n");

}
```

Break statement as a control statement for the Java programming language

Break statement is one of the few control statements Java give to control the stream of the program. As the name says, Break Statement is commonly used to break the loop of switch statement.

Duly noting that Java does not give Go To statement like other programming languages e.g. C, C++. Break statement has two structures marked and unlabeled. The Unlabeled Break statement is the type of break statement which is utilized to hop out of the loop when a particular condition happens. This type of break statement is additionally utilized as a part of the switch statement.

See below example:

```
for(int var =0; var < 5 ; var++)
{
      System.out.println( "Var is :  " + var);
              if(var == 3)
                      break;
}
```

In the above break statement illustration, control will hop out of the loop when var progresses toward becoming three (3).

Labeled Break Statement

The unlabeled adaptation of the break statement is utilized when we need to bounce out of a solitary loop or a single case in a switch statement. Named variant of the break statement is utilized when we need to swing out of a settled or numerous loops. See below sample:

```
Outer:
for(int var1=0; var1 < 5 ; var1++)
{
            for(int var2 = 1; var2 < 5; var2++)
            {
        System.out.println( "var1:" + var1 + ", var2:" + var2);
                        if(var1 == 3)
                                    break Outer;
            }
}
```

Utilization of Break statements for Java programming

The break statement in Java programming language has the accompanying two utilizations. At the point when the break statement is experienced inside a loop, the loop is quickly ended, and the program control resumes at the following statement taking after the loop. It can be utilized to end a case in the switch statement. The syntax of a break is a solitary statement inside any loop.

The flow diagram

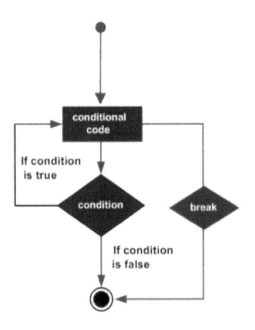

Example:

```
public class Test {

  public static void main(String args[]) {
    int [] numbers = {10, 20, 30, 40, 50};

    for(int x : numbers ) {
      if( x == 30 ) {
        break;
      }
      System.out.print( x );
      System.out.print("\n");
    }
  }}
```

Producing an output of ten (10) and twenty (20) respectively,
What methods are and how to write them

Defining methods

A method in Java has the following as elements that are required which are the following:
- Open and close brackets
- Method Name
- Return type
- Body of statements located in between brackets

A method declaration contains the following six components/parts:

1. Modifiers
2. Return type
3. Method name
4. Parameter list
5. The exception list
6. Method body

Below is another example of a common method declaration that has all 6 components:

```
public double calculateAnswer(double wingSpan, int numberOfEngines,
                              double length, double grossTons) {
    //do the calculation here
}
```

How to Make Method Names

You can use any word as a name for any method you
will include in your code as long as it is a legal identifier
– this means that it isn't a reserved word in Java programming. However, you should be aware of certain
coding conventions (note that a lot of programming languages have naming conventions).

Note that in Java programming, the usual naming
convention is to use verbs to name a Method. Method
names should be in lowercase letters. It can also be a
multi-word name provided that the first word is a verb
and it is in all lowercase. Below is an example of method
names.

```
run
runFast
getBackground
getFinalData
compareTo
setX
isEmpty
```

Usually, a method has a special name inside its class.
In any case, a method may have an indistinguishable
name from different methods because of method
overloading.

CHAPTER 5

METHOD OVERLOADING

Method overloading is supported in the Java programming language. Each method will be recognized by Java with the use of various method signatures. A class can have several methods with similar names as long as the parameter list of each method differs from each other.

One good example is when a class uses calligraphy to draw the different types of data. The class will consist of a method that will be executed to draw each type of data whether they are integers, strings, etc. It would be tedious to use a different unique name for each method in a class like drawFloat, draw Integer, drawString, and others more.

Fortunately, in the Java language, all the methods for drawing can have similar names. Just make sure that each method has passed a different list of arguments. Therefore, the class may contain four different methods with similar name – draw. However, each of the four methods should have a parameter list that is different from each other.

```
public class DataArtist {
    ...
    public void draw(String s) {
        ...
    }
    public void draw(int i) {
        ...
    }
    public void draw(double f) {
        ...
    }
    public void draw(int i, double f) {
        ...
    }
}
```

To differentiate overloaded methods from one another, Java compiler will look into the type and the number of passed arguments that each method has. As seen from the above example, draw(int i) and draw(String s) have different types of argument. Thus, these methods are different from each other.

The Java compiler will not be able to differentiate overloaded methods if you declare two or more methods to have similar names and similar type and number of passed arguments.

The Java compiler will not use the return type to differentiate overloaded methods. Therefore it is erroneous to declare two or more methods to have similar signatures even if their return type is different from each other.

Writing a method

In Java, an accumulation of articulations that are gathered together to layout an operation is called a method. In the instance where the code includes System.out.println() method, for instance, that part of the code will then execute the included lines of code on its block to display output to the screen.

You can actually create methods that can return values (or not), make a method with or without parameters, and make use of method abstraction as you design your entire code.

Consider line below; this syntax is how you declare a method in Java. This creates two int type variables that are declared in the code as "a" and "b":

```
public static int methodName(int a, int b) {
    // body
}
```

In the syntax above "int" is the returnType, which means a method can return a value – as stated earlier, you can make methods in Java that do not have a returnType.
"public static" in this syntax refers to the modifier. This tells us the access type used by this Method. "methodname" on the other hand is the user supplied name of the method construct. As stated earlier, "a" and "b" are the parameters listed – again they are also user supplied.

Method definition in Java will include a method header and a method body. See the standard syntax structure below:

```
modifier returnType nameOfMethod (Parameter List) {
    // method body
}
```

As explained earlier the "modifier" is the access type that will be used by the method. The "method body" will include the statements that will be executed and it will define what the method will do with these included statements. The "returnType" defines whether the method will return a value or not. The "Parameter List" is a list of parameters and it will define the number of parameters to be used, their order, and the data type that will be used as well.

Note that the variables in this syntax are always user defined. Again, please remember that a method may have zero parameters. The part of the syntax called "NameOfMethod" is a user supplied name.

Here is another example of a method definition in Java:

```
/** the snippet returns the minimum between two numbers */
public static int minFunction(int n1, int n2) {
    int min;
    if (n1 > n2)
        min = n2;
    else
        min = n1;

    return min; }
```

The method above will return an int type value. This method also declares two parameters namely n1 and n2. If you follow the code for the body of the method, you can deduce that it will return the smaller value between the two parameters that have been declared in the syntax header.

Calling a Method in Java

You need to call a method for it to be used in the code. You can call a method using either one of these two ways – it has no return value (returning nothing), or it returns a value.

Method calling is pretty simple to execute. Once a program calls a method, the called method gets the full control of the program. There are two specific conditions in which the called method returns the full control to the program (its caller). One, the called method has reached its closing brace and two, the called method has already executed the return statement.

A method that is returning with nothing will execute another statement. See the examples below.

```
System.out.println("This is tutorialspoint.com!");
```

See below example to understand the method return value.

```
int result = sum(6, 9);
```

The below example demonstrates the procedure on how to call and define a method.

Example:

```java
public class ExampleMinNumber {

    public static void main(String[] args) {
        int a = 11;
        int b = 6;
        int c = minFunction(a, b);
        System.out.println("Minimum Value = " + c);
    }

    /** returns the minimum of two numbers */
    public static int minFunction(int n1, int n2) {
        int min;
        if (n1 > n2)
            min = n2;
        else
            min = n1;

        return min;
    }}
```

The produced output is Minimum value = 6.

The definition of void keyword

As mentioned earlier, there are methods in Java programming that return nothing or no value. You need to use a void keyword to make these methods. As seen in the example below, the void keyword used is methodRankPoints. As a void called method, it will be returning nothing. The Java statement in the example that calls for the void method is methodRankPoints(255.7);. Every Java statement should end with a semicolon (;).

```
public class ExampleVoid {

    public static void main(String[] args) {
        methodRankPoints(255.7);
    }

    public static void methodRankPoints(double points) {
        if (points >= 202.5) {
            System.out.println("Rank:A1");
        }else if (points >= 122.4) {
            System.out.println("Rank:A2");
        }else {
            System.out.println("Rank:A3");
        }
    }}
```

Passing parameters by value

When you are in the process of calling a method, arguments have to be passed. The passing parameters should be within the specifications of the called method. Passing parameters can be either by reference or by value.

When there are certain parameters involved when calling a method, it is known as the Passing Parameters by Value. With the presence of these passing parameters, the value of the argument is now passed to these parameters.

Shown below is an example of a code that uses passing parameters by value. As you can see, the argument values didn't change at all even after the calling of the method is executed.

Example:

```
public class swappingExample {

   public static void main(String[] args) {
      int a = 30;
      int b = 45;
      System.out.println("Before swapping, a = " + a + " and b = " + b);

      // Invoke the swap method
      swapFunction(a, b);
      System.out.println("\n**Now, Before and After swapping values will
be same here**:");
      System.out.println("After swapping, a = " + a + " and b is " + b);
   }

   public static void swapFunction(int a, int b) {
      System.out.println("Before swapping(Inside), a = " + a + " b = " +
b);

      // Swap n1 with n2
      int c = a;
      a = b;
      b = c;
      System.out.println("After swapping(Inside), a = " + a + " b = " +
b);
   }}
```

Producing the output in the illustration below:

```
Before swapping, a = 30 and b = 45
Before swapping(Inside), a = 30 b = 45
After swapping(Inside), a = 45 b = 30

**Now, Before and After swapping values will be same here**:
After swapping, a = 30 and b is 45
```

Utilizing command-line arguments

During manipulation of calling process, arguments are to be passed. These ought to be in an indistinguishable request from their separate parameters in the particular method. Parameters can be passed by reference or by value.

When passing Parameters by Value implies calling a method with a parameter, because of that, the argument value is transmitted to the parameter. The below example demonstrates a case of passing parameter by value. The estimations of the argument continue as before even after the method summon.

Example:

```java
public class CommandLine {

   public static void main(String args[]) {
      for(int i = 0; i<args.length; i++) {
         System.out.println("args[" + i + "]: " +  args[i]);
      }
   }}
```

Execute the below program,

```
$java CommandLine this is a command line 200 -100
```

that will yield the output below:

```
args[0]: this
args[1]: is
args[2]: a
args[3]: command
args[4]: line
args[5]: 200
args[6]: -100
```

Constructors

A constructor introduces a variable when it is made. It has an indistinguishable name from its class and is linguistically like a method. Contractors are used to perform many execution procedures in pursuance of creating a fully formed object.

Usually, the user will utilize a constructor to give introductory values to the variables characterized by the class or to play out some other startup methodology required to make a full-fledged object.

All classes have constructors, regardless of whether you characterize one or not, on the grounds that Java naturally gives a default constructor that instates all part factors to zero. As it may, once you characterize your own particular constructor, the default constructor shall never be utilized in the future. Below is a straightforward example that uses a constructor without parameters,

Example:

```
// A simple constructor.class MyClass {
    int x;

    // Following is the constructor
    MyClass() {
        x = 10;
    }}
```

Use a contractor to start-up objects (see below example)

```
public class ConsDemo {

    public static void main(String args[]) {
        MyClass t1 = new MyClass();
        MyClass t2 = new MyClass();
        System.out.println(t1.x + " " + t2.x);
}}
```

yielding the output 10 10.

Parameterized Constructor

Usually, the user will require a constructor that acknowledges at least one parameters. Parameters are added to a constructor similarly that they are added to a method, simply pronounce them inside the enclosures after the constructor's name. The below example is a basic illustration that uses a constructor with a parameter.

Example:

```
// A simple constructor.class MyClass {
    int x;

    // Following is the constructor
    MyClass(int i ) {
        x = i;
}}
```

calling a constructor to start-up objects (see below example).

Example:

```
public class ConsDemo {

    public static void main(String args[]) {
        MyClass t1 = new MyClass( 10 );
        MyClass t2 = new MyClass( 20 );
        System.out.println(t1.x + " " + t2.x);
}}
```

Producing the output ten twenty (10 20).

This keyword

"this" is a keyword in Java which is utilized as a kind of perspective to the object of the present class, within an example method or a constructor. Utilizing this you can suggest the parts from a class, for example, constructors, methods, and variables. The keyword this is utilized just inside constructors or instance methods.

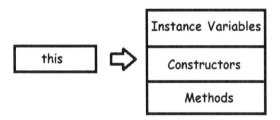

Typically, the keyword this is utilized to separate the example factors from local variables on the chance that they have same names, inside a constructor or a method.

Example:

```
class Student {
    int age;
    Student(int age) {
        this.age = age;
}}
```

The user can call one type of constructor whether default or parameterized constructor from another in a class. The such is called as explicit constructor command.

Example:

```
class Student {
    int age
    Student() {
        this(20);
    }

    Student(int age) {
        this.age = age;
}}
```

Here is an illustration that uses this keyword to get to the individuals from a class. Duplicate and glue the given program in a record with the name (This_Example.java).

Example:

```java
public class This_Example {
   // Instance variable num
   int num = 10;

   This_Example() {
      System.out.println("This is an example program on keyword this");
   }

   This_Example(int num) {
      // Invoking the default constructor
      this();

      // Assigning the local variable num to the instance variable num
      this.num = num;
   }

   public void greet() {
      System.out.println("Hi Welcome to Tutorialspoint");
   }

   public void print() {
      // Local variable num
      int num = 20;

      // Printing the local variable
      System.out.println("value of local variable num is : "+num);

      // Printing the instance variable
      System.out.println("value of instance variable num is : "+this.num);

      // Invoking the greet method of a class
      this.greet();
   }

   public static void main(String[] args) {
      // Instantiating the class
      This_Example obj1 = new This_Example();

      // Invoking the print method
      obj1.print();

      // Passing a new value to the num variable through parametrized
constructor
      This_Example obj2 = new This_Example(30);

      // Invoking the print method again
      obj2.print();
   }}
```

Yielding the output below:

```
This is an example program on keyword this
value of local variable num is : 20
value of instance variable num is : 10
Hi Welcome to Tutorialspoint
This is an example program on keyword this
value of local variable num is : 20
value of instance variable num is : 30
Hi Welcome to Tutorialspoint
```

var-args

Variable arguments (var-args) JDK 1.5 empowers you to pass a variable number of arguments of a similar class to a method. The parameter in the method is proclaimed as follows. In the method presentation, the user indicates the class taken after by an ellipsis (...). Just a single variable-length parameter might be indicated in a method, and this parameter must be the last parameter. Any consistent parameters must go before it.

Example:

```java
public class VarargsDemo {

    public static void main(String args[]) {
        // Call method with variable args
        printMax(34, 3, 3, 2, 56.5);
        printMax(new double[] {1, 2, 3});
    }

    public static void printMax( double... numbers) {
        if (numbers.length == 0) {
            System.out.println("No argument passed");
            return;
        }

        double result = numbers[0];

        for(int i = 1; i <    numbers.length; i++)
        if (numbers[i] >    result)
        result = numbers[i];
        System.out.println("The max value is " + result);
    }
}
```

Producing the outputs Output "The max value is 56.5" and "the max value is 3.0."

The finalize( ) Method

It is conceivable to characterize a method that will be called just before an object's last demolition. This method is called finalize( ), and it can be utilized to guarantee that an object terminates neatly. For instance, you may utilize finalize( ) to ensure that an open record claimed by that object is shut. To add a finalizer to a class, you basically characterize the finalized( ) method. The Java runtime calls that method at whatever point it is going to reuse an object of that class.

Inside the finalize( ) method, the user will determine those activities that must be performed before an object is annihilated. The finalize( ) method has the following general frame. the keyword secured is a specifier that forestalls access to finalize( ) by code characterized outside its class. This implies you can't know when or regardless of the possibility that finalize( ) will be executed. For instance, if your program closes before junk gathering happens, finalize( ) won't execute.

The general form of the finalize() method

```
protected void finalize( ) {
    // finalization code here
}
```

Straightforward Java Method

At times the terms capacity and method are utilized reciprocally. They are basically the same. The right phrasing for Java is method. It is an arrangement of summons that can be utilized over again. They share similitudes with sub routines at the beginning of programming. The things that the user shall need when starting to utilize Java method are a Java Compiler, and a fundamental Java knowledge

A basic Java method requires at least three things: Perceivability Return Type(e.g. void, int, twofold, etc.), and name (the necessities to call a method).

Visibility implies who can get to it. On the chance that it is open, any individual who approaches your class record can get to the method. In a few conditions, this is splendidly fine. In the event that the method is private, just the capacities within that class can call the method. This is utilized as utility methods to accomplish something you don't need just any individual who utilizes the class to do.

49

Return type is void in the event that you don't need the method to give you any data back. It would be utilized for such things as a method that prints out something. Some other return requires an arrival proclamation with the sort of information it returns. For instance, on the off chance that you include two whole numbers and need the after effects of that integer, the user's return type would be int.

Name of the method is anything you pick that is not effectively utilized as a part of the class unless you are over-burdening the method which is past the extent of this section.

On the chance that you need the method to accomplish something with the data you supply it, you additionally need to incorporate parameters inside the ( ) You incorporate what data type it is and give that parameter a name when you are announcing a local factor for that only method).

CHAPTER 6

THE WHAT, HOW, AND WHY
OF ARRAYS

Arrays

When there is a multiply subscripted collections of numeric data entries, then you have an array. To create and handle arrays, there is an easier way to do them, most especially the matrices.

When you see a non-negative integers vector, it is called as a dimension vector. An array is a k-dimensional array when its length is k. For example, a matrix is considered as a two-dimensional array. Its dimensions are indexed based on the given values of the dimension vector.

A vector will become an array provided that its dim attribute is a dimension vector. As shown in the example below, z is a dimension vector of 1500 elements.

A vector can be used by R as an array only if it has a dimension vector as its dim attribute. Suppose, for example, z is a vector of 1500 elements. The assignment

> dim(z) <- c(3,5,100)

51

51

gives it the dim attribute that allows it to be treated as a 3 by 5 by 100 array.

Other functions such as matrix() and array() are available for simpler and more natural looking assignments, as we shall see in Section 5.4 [The array() function], page 20.

The values in the data vector give the values in the array in the same order as they would occur in FORTRAN, that is "column major order," with the first subscript moving fastest and the last subscript slowest.

For example if the dimension vector for an array, say a, is c(3,4,2) then there are 3 4 2 = 24 entries in a and the data vector holds them in the order a[1,1,1], a[2,1,1], ..., a[2,4,2], a[3,4,2].

Arrays can be one-dimensional: such arrays are usually treated in the same way as vectors (including when printing), but the exceptions can cause confusion.[1]

Array indexing. Subsections of an array

Individual elements of an array may be referenced by giving the name of the array followed by the subscripts in square brackets, separated by commas.

More generally, subsections of an array may be specified by giving a sequence of index vectors in place of subscripts; however if any index position is given an

---

[1] W. N. Venables, D. M. Smith and the R Core Team. An Introduction to R, Notes on R: A Programming Environment for Data Analysis and Graphics Version 3.4.0 . Retrieved (2017-04-21)

empty index vector, then the full range of that subscript is taken.

Continuing the previous example, a[2,,] is a 4 2 array with dimension vector c(4,2) and data vector containing the values

c(a[2,1,1], a[2,2,1], a[2,3,1], a[2,4,1], a[2,1,2], a[2,2,2], a[2,3,2], a[2,4,2])

in that order. a[,,] stands for the entire array, which is the same as omitting the subscripts entirely and using a alone.

For any array, say Z, the dimension vector may be referenced explicitly as dim(Z) (on either side of an assignment).

Also, if an array name is given with just one subscript or index vector, then the corresponding values of the data vector only are used; in this case, the dimension vector is ignored. This is not the case, however, if the single index is not a vector but itself an array, as we next discuss.

The array() function

As well as giving a vector structure a dim attribute, arrays can be constructed from vectors by the array function, which has the form

```
> Z <- array(data_vector, dim_vector)
```

For example, if the vector h contains 24 or fewer, numbers then the command

```
> Z <- array(h, dim=c(3,4,2))
```

would use h to set up 3 by 4 by 2 array in Z. If the size of h is exactly 24, the result is the same as

> Z <- h ; dim(Z) <- c(3,4,2)[2]

However if h is shorter than 24, its values are recycled from the beginning again to make it up to size 24 (see Section 5.4.1 [The recycling rule], page 20) but dim(h) <- c(3,4,2) would signal an error about mismatching length. As an extreme but common example

> Z <- array(0, c(3,4,2))

makes Z an array of all zeros.

At this point dim(Z) stands for the dimension vector c(3,4,2), and Z[1:24] stands for the data vector as it was in h, and Z[] with an empty subscript or Z with no subscript stands for the entire array as an array.

Arrays may be used in arithmetic expressions, and the result is an array formed by element-by-element operations on the data vector. The dim attributes of operands generally need to be the same, and this becomes the dimension vector of the result. So if A, B and C are all similar arrays, then

> D <- 2*A*B + C + 1

D is also a similar array based on the element-by-element operations as shown above. This is just the basics.

---

[2] W. N. Venables, D. M. Smith and the R Core Team. An Introduction to R, Notes on R: A Programming Environment for Data Analysis and Graphics Version 3.4.0 . Retrieved (2017-04-21)

The exact ruling with regards to vector calculations and mixed arrays will need to be studied deeper.

The Rule of Recycling Array Arithmetic and Mixed Vector

We will be having a hard time if we will try to search in the references about the exact ruling that will affect the element-by-element calculations of mixed arrays and vectors. Listed below are what we consider to be a reliable guide basing from our experiences.

- The expression is scanned from left to right.

- Any short vector operands are extended by recycling their values until they match the size of any other operands.

- As long as short vectors and arrays only are encountered, the arrays must all have the same dim attribute or an error results.

- Any vector operand longer than a matrix or array operand generates an error.

- If array structures are present and no error or coercion to vector has been precipitated, the result is an array structure with the common dim attribute of its array operands.

Two Arrays' Outer Product

The outer product is an essential operation on arrays. The outer product of the two numeric arrays a and b is also an array. However, its dimension vector is derived by joining together each of their dimension vectors. It is important to retain the order of the dimension vectors.

The data vector is derived from all the possible formation of the [3]products of elements of a's data vector with those of b's. We use the symbol %o% as the special operator for the outer product.

> ab <- a %o% b

An alternative is

> ab <- outer(a, b, "*")

The multiplication function can be replaced by an arbitrary function of two variables. For example, if we wished to evaluate the function $f(x; y) = \cos(y)=(1 + x2)$ over a regular grid of values with x- and y-coordinates defined by the R vectors x and y respectively, we could proceed as follows:

f <- function(x, y) cos(y)/(1 + x^2)

z <- outer(x, y, f)

In particular, the outer product of two ordinary vectors is a doubly subscripted array (that is a matrix, of rank at most 1). Notice that the outer product operator is of course noncommutative. Defining your own R functions will be considered further in Chapter 10 [Writing your own functions], page 42.

An example: Determinants of 2 by 2 single-digit matrices

---

[3] W. N. Venables, D. M. Smith and the R Core Team. An Introduction to R, Notes on R: A Programming Environment for Data Analysis and Graphics Version 3.4.0 . Retrieved (2017-04-21)

As an artificial but cute example, consider the determinants of 2 by 2 matrices [a; b; c; d] where each entry is a non-negative integer in the range 0; 1; : : : ; 9, that is a digit.

The problem is to find the determinants, ad bc, of all possible matrices of this form and represent the frequency with which each value occurs as a high-density plot. This amounts to finding the probability distribution of the determinant if each digit is chosen independently and uniformly at random.

A neat way of doing this uses the outer() function twice:

d <- outer(0:9, 0:9)

fr <- table(outer(d, d, "-"))

plot(fr, xlab="Determinant", ylab="Frequency")

Notice that plot() here uses a histogram like a plot method because it "sees" that fr is of class "table." The "obvious" way of doing this problem with for loops, to be discussed in Chapter 9 [Loops and conditional execution], page 40, is so inefficient as to be impractical.

It is also perhaps surprising that about 1 in 20 such matrices is singular.

Generalized transpose of an array

The function aperm(a, perm) may be used to permute an array, a. The argument perm must be a permutation of the integers fl; : : : ; kg, where k is the number of subscripts in a. The result of the function is an array of the same size as a but with old dimension given by perm[j] becoming the new j-th dimension. The easiest way to think of this operation is as a generalization of transposition for matrices. Indeed if A is a matrix, (that is, a doubly subscripted array) then B given by

> B <- aperm(A, c(2,1))

is just the transpose of A. For this special case a simpler function t() is available, so we could have used B <- t(A).

The concatenation function, c(), with arrays

It should be noted that whereas cbind() and rbind() are concatenation functions that respect dim attributes, the basic c() function does not, but rather clears numeric objects of all dim and dimnames attributes. This is occasionally useful in its own right.

The official way to coerce an array back to a simple vector object is to use as.vector()

> vec <- as.vector(X)

However, a similar result can be achieved by using c() with just one argument, simply for this side-effect:

> vec <- c(X)

There are slight differences between the two, but ultimately the choice between them is largely a matter of style (with the former being preferable).[4]

---

[4] W. N. Venables, D. M. Smith and the R Core Team. An Introduction to R, Notes on R: A Programming Environment for Data Analysis and Graphics Version 3.4.0 . Retrieved (2017-04-21)

Creating an array in Java

Creating an array in Java involves three steps:

1. Declare the array name.
2. Create the array.
3. Initialize the array values.

An array element is defined by putting its index in square brackets after the array name: the code a[i] alludes to element I of the array a[]. For instance, the accompanying code makes an array of n quantities of the type to be twofold or doubled, all introduced to zero (0):

```
double[] a;              // declare the array
a = new double[n];       // create the array
for (int i = 0; i < n; i++)   // elements are indexed from 0 to n-1
   a[i] = 0.0;           // initialize all elements to 0.0
```

Generally used array processing code

When the user uses the "ArrayExamples.java," it will lead the user towards a list of typical examples of using arrays in Java.

| *create an array with random values* | ```java
double[] a = new double[n];
for (int i = 0; i < n; i++)
    a[i] = Math.random();
``` |
| *print the array values, one per line* | ```java
for (int i = 0; i < n; i++)
    System.out.println(a[i]);
``` |
| *find the maximum of the array values* | ```java
double max = Double.NEGATIVE_INFINITY;
for (int i = 0; i < n; i++)
    if (a[i] > max) max = a[i];
``` |
| *compute the average of the array values* | ```java
double sum = 0.0;
for (int i = 0; i < n; i++)
    sum += a[i];
double average = sum / n;
``` |
| *reverse the values within an array* | ```java
for (int i = 0; i < n/2; i++)
{
    double temp = a[i];
    a[i] = a[n-1-i];
    a[n-i-1] = temp;
}
``` |
| *copy sequence of values to another array* | ```java
double[] b = new double[n];
for (int i = 0; i < n; i++)
    b[i] = a[i];
``` |

Array programming

The user must consider some important factors of programming with Arrays.

➤ Array length. The length of an array is fixed prior to its creation. The user can know the length of an array in the program by using the code a.length.

➤ zero-based indexing. The user must always specify to the 1st element of an array a[] as a[0], the second as a[1], the third as a [2], the fourth as a [3] and so on. It is more convenient and natural for the user to define the 1st element as a[1], the 2nd value as a[2], the third as a[3] and so on. However starting the indexing with zero has few advantages and has developed as the typivsl used in present day programming languages.

> Default array initialization. For a thrift in code, we regularly exploit Java's default array start up tradition. For instance, the accompanying statement is equal to the four lines of code at the highest point of this page:

```
double[] a = new double[n];
```

The usual The starting value is zero (0) for all statistical primitive and false for type.

> Memory representation. also known as memory allocation, it is the procedure when you utilize new to make an array, Java saves space in memory for it and introduces the values.

> Bounds checking. When programming with arrays,the user should be cautious. It is the programmer's duty to utilize legal files while getting to an array element.

> Setting array values at compile time. When the user has few strict values that he or she needs to keep in the array, he or she can introduce it by posting the qualities between wavy braces, isolated by a comma.

For instance, the programmer may utilize the

following code in a program that practices playing cards.

```
String[] SUITS = {
    "Clubs", "Diamonds", "Hearts", "Spades"
};

String[] RANKS = {
    "2", "3", "4", "5", "6", "7", "8", "9", "10",
    "Jack", "Queen", "King", "Ace"
};
```

After the creation of the two arrays, the user might utilize the arrays to print an arbitrary card name like the Queen of Clubs, see below example:

```
String[] deck = new String[RANKS.length * SUITS.length];
for (int i = 0; i < RANKS.length; i++)
    for (int j = 0; j < SUITS.length; j++)
        deck[SUITS.length*i + j] = RANKS[i] + " of " + SUITS[j];
System.out.println(RANKS[i] + " of " + SUITS[j]);
```

Setting array values at run time. Setting array values at run time. A more average circumstance is the point at which the user wishes to process the qualities to be put away in an array. An example is the time when the user may utilize the accompanying code to introduce an array of length fifty-two (52) that exhibit to a deck of playing cards, utilizing the arrays SUITS[] and RANKS[].

```
double[] harmonic = new double[n];
for (int i = 1; i < n; i++)
    harmonic[i] = harmonic[i-1] + 1.0/i;
```

Sampling and shuffling

The programmer should now portray some helpful algorithms for revising the elements in an array. Habitually, the reader would wish to trade two values in an array. Proceeding with the case with playing cards, the accompanying code trades the card at position i and the card at position j: Rearranging, the accompanying code rearranges the deck of cards:

```
String temp = deck[i];
deck[i] = deck[j];
deck[j] = temp;
```

Continuing from left to right, we pick an irregular card from deck[i] through deck[n-1] (each card similarly likely) and trade it with deck[i]. This code is more refined than it may appear: see the reading material for points of interest. Deck.java has the full code for making and rearranging a deck of cards.

Sampling or testing without substitution. Much of the time, is when the user needs to draw an arbitrary example from a set with the end goal that every individual from the set shows up at least once in the specimen. Sample.java takes two order line contentions m and n and makes a change of length n whose first m sections include an irregular example. See the reading material for subtle elements.

Precomputed values

Precomputed values are one straightforward use of arrays, to spare values that the reader figured, for later utilization. For instance, assume that you are composing a program that performs figurings utilizing little estimations of the harmoic numbers. One simple approach to finish such an errand is to spare the qualities in an array with the code below. See below example.

Example:

```
double[] harmonic = new double[n];
for (int i = 1; i < n; i++)
    harmonic[i] = harmonic[i-1] + 1.0/i;
```

and afterward basically utilize the code harmonic[i] to exemplify to any of the qualities. Precomputing values along these lines in a case of a space-time barter. Putting resources into space, in order to spare the values. The programmer can save time since the user needs not to recompute them. This technique is not viable on the chance that we require values for colossal n. However, it is extremely powerful on the chance that we require countless values for little n.

Cutting down repetitive code

Another straightforward use of arrays, consider the following code piece, which prints the name of a month given its number like,one for January, three for March, et cetera:

```
if        (m ==  1) System.out.println("Jan");
else if (m ==  2) System.out.println("Feb");
else if (m ==  3) System.out.println("Mar");
else if (m ==  4) System.out.println("Apr");
else if (m ==  5) System.out.println("May");
else if (m ==  6) System.out.println("Jun");
else if (m ==  7) System.out.println("Jul");
else if (m ==  8) System.out.println("Aug");
else if (m ==  9) System.out.println("Sep");
else if (m == 10) System.out.println("Oct");
else if (m == 11) System.out.println("Nov");
else if (m == 12) System.out.println("Dec");
```

The writer may use a switch statement. However, there is a much efficient solid alternative. To use an array of strings having the initial names of each month, boast as a more convenient method.

```
String[] MONTHS = {
    "", "Jan", "Feb", "Mar", "Apr", "May", "Jun",
    "Jul", "Aug", "Sep", "Oct", "Nov", "Dec"
};
...
System.out.println(MONTHS[m]);
```

This procedure would be particularly helpful in the event that the user expected to get to the name of a month by its number in a few better places inside the program. Taking note that the readers purposefully squander one opening in the array element zero(0) to transform MONTHS[1] compare to January, as needed.

Two-dimensional arrays in Java

In numerous applications, a characteristic approach to compose data is to utilize a table of numbers sorted out in a rectangle and to allude to lines and sections in the table. The scientific deliberation comparing to such tables is a lattice. The relating Java build is a two-dimensional array.

Two-dimensional arrays in Java, refer to the element in segment j and in line i of a 2D array a[][], we utilize the documentation a[i][j]; to proclaim a 2D array, the user must include another combination of brackets; in order to make the array. The user can determine the quantity of lines taken after by the quantity of segments.

Java string array tutorial

Some users encounter difficulty in remembering Java array syntax. Some methods are using and declaring Java string arrays.

> Sizing, declaring, and utilizing a string array.
A)The first step is to declare the Java string array.
B)Second is to utilize the Java string array.

The user can declare a Java string array inside the body of a class, see below example.
Example:
```
private String[] fruits = new String[20];
```

The user can now add the elements to the brand new string array.
```
fruits[0] = "apple";
fruits[1] = "banana";
fruits[3] = "orange";
```

66

> Declaring the array string size
  The first step involves declaring without revealing
the   size.

Example:

```
private String[] fruits;
```

The programmer is constructing a reference named fruits, and adding it to the array (see below example). The specification of the size of the string array shall be tackled in the succeeding steps.
Example:

```
fruits = new String[20];
fruits[0] = "apple";
fruits[1] = "banana";
fruits[3] = "orange";
```

> Completely defining the Java string array with
just   one step.

A similar method to create a Java string array is to populate and declare the array in just one step. See the below syntax sample.
Example:
// declare and populate a java string array
String[] formData = {
  "apple"
  "banana"
  "orange"
};

> Creating a two-dimensional (2D) Java String array

Taking an example from the Java/Swing prototype populating a JTable.

Example:

```
// a 2d java string array
Object[][] data = {
  {"CUSTOMER REP", "JOHN ELWAY",    "1001" },
  {"TECH SERVICE", " PEYTON MANNING", "1002" },
  {"TECH SERVICE", " TOM BRADY",     "1003" },
  {"ACCOUNTING",  "FRED FLINSTONE", "1004" }
};
```

Steps:

a) Creating a Java 2D array

b) Assigning the array of strings beside the Java string

c) Finding a reference inside the classes of Java Object type

The technique shown above would be a handy way if the 2D array contained varied types of Java objects. These methods represent the processes of iterating over a String array using a Java five for loop.

How to sort and search arrays

The sorting issue is to modify an array of things in an ascending order. In this segment, we will consider in detail two traditional ways for sorting and searching. The binary pursuit and mergesort alongside a few applications where their productivity assumes a basic part.

Binary search

A powerful system is to keep up an interval that contains the mystery number, figure the number amidst the interim, and afterward utilize the response to divide the interval size. Questions.java executes this procedure. It is a case of the common problem-solving method a technique known as binary search.See example below.

Example:

interval	length	Q	A
0 ————————————————— 128	128	≥ 64 ?	true
0 ——— 64 ————————— 128	64	≥ 96 ?	false
0 ——— 64 ——— 96	32	≥ 80 ?	false
0 ——— 64 — 80	16	≥ 72 ?	true
0 ——— 72 — 80	8	≥ 76 ?	true
0 ——— 76 — 80	4	≥ 78 ?	false
0 ——— 76 78	2	≥ 77 ?	true
0 ——— 77	1	= 77	

Insertion sort

Insertion sort. Insertion sort is a savage sorting method that depends on a basic technique that individuals regularly use to orchestrate hands of playing cards. Consider the cards each one in turn and embed each into its legitimate place among those officially permitted, keeping them sorted. The accompanying code impersonates this procedure in a Java strategy that sorts strings in an array. See below example.

Example:

```
public static void sort(String[] a) {
    int n = a.length;
    for (int i = 1; i < n; i++) {
        for (int j = i; j > 0; j--) {
            if (a[j-1].compareTo(a[j]) > 0)
                exch(a, j, j-1);
            else break;
        }
    }
}
```

Mergesort

Mergesort builds up a quicker sorting strategy, the user utilizes a partition and overcomes a way to deal with calculation outline that each software engineer needs to acquire. To mergesort an array, we partition it into two parts, sort the two parts autonomously, and afterward consolidate the outcomes to sort the full array. To sort a[lo, hey), we utilize the accompanying recursive system. Merge.java is a usage of this procedure. Here is a hint of the substance of the array during a fission or merging.

Frequency counts

FrequencyCount.java peruses a grouping of strings from standard data input, and after that prints a table of the particular values found and the quantity of times each was found, in descending frequencies. The user achieves this by two sorts.

The initial step is to sort the strings on standard information. For this situation, we are less keen on the way that the strings are put into sorted style, however in the way that sorting units break even with strings. In the event that the data input is:

70

Example:

to be or not to be to

The sort resulting to:

be be not or to to to

The Counter.java data sort that we considered is the ideal apparatus for the given task.

Next, the user must group the objects. One has the ability to do as such with no unique plans since Counter executes the Comparable interface.

The application highlighted in FrequencyCount.java is a basic phonetic examination. Which terms often sprouts in a content. A marvel known as Zipf's law says that the recurrence of the ith most successive word in a content of m unmistakable words is corresponding to $1/i$.

Importance of the array sorting and searching procedures

Logical case of sorting. Google show query items in diving outcomes a "significance," a spreadsheet shows segments sorted by a specific field, Matlab sorts the genuine eigenvalues of a symmetric grid in diving products. Sorting likewise emerges as a basic subroutine in numerous applications that seem to have nothing to do with sorting at all including, data compression, computer visuals, computational science, production network administration, and social decision and voting, Historically, sorting was most essential for business applications, however sorting additionally assumes a noteworthy part in the logical figuring foundation. NASA and the liquids mechanics group utilize sorting to study issues in tenuous stream; these impact recognition issues are particularly testing since they include ten of billions of particles and must be comprehended on supercomputers in parallel. Comparable sorting strategies are utilized as a part of some quick N-body recreation codes. Another critical logical use of sorting is for load adjusting the processors of parallel supercomputers. Researchers depend on smart sorting calculation to perform load-adjusting on such frameworks.

CHAPTER 7
LISTS

Lists

When you have an object that is composed of an ordered set of objects; and this ordered set is used as the main object's components then this construct is what is known as a list.

The components don't have to be composed of similar types or modes. A list can be composed of a function, a complex vector, a logical value, a numeric vector, a character array, a matrix, and so forth. Below is an example of a simple list.

Each component must be numbered, and these numbers will be used to refer to and identify each component of a list. If the name of your list is Lst and it is composed of four components, then each component will be separately referred to as Lst[[1]], Lst[[2]], Lst[[3]] and Lst[[4]]. If one of your components is a vector subscripted array, let's say, the fourth component Lst[[4]], then the first entry should be Lst[[4]][1].

length(Lst) is a function that will identify how many components in the top level does your Lst list have.

You can name the components of your lists. You can use a character string for the component name instead of the usual numbers found in the double square brackets. You can also use the expression

> name$component_name

and it is still the same.

Using the component's name is very helpful in remembering the items in your list especially if you are forgetful when it comes to numbers.

Below is an example of what is mentioned above.

Lst[["name"]] is the format to use when you want to use the component's names in your list inside the double square brackets. You can use this in instances wherein the component's name that is to be used is stored as a variable in another list.

> x <- "name"; Lst[[x]]

It is very important to distinguish Lst[[1]] from Lst[1]. '[[...]]' is the operator used to select a single element, whereas '[...]' is a general subscripting operator. Thus the former is the first object in the list Lst, and if it is a named list the name is not included. The latter is a sublist of the list Lst consisting of the first entry only. If it is a named list, the names are transferred to the sublist.

The names of components may be abbreviated down to the minimum number of letters needed to identify them uniquely. Thus Lst$coefficients may be minimally specified as Lst$coe and Lst$covariance as Lst$cov.

The vector of names is in fact simply an attribute of the list like any other and may be handled as such. Other structures besides lists may, of course, similarly be given a names attribute also.

Constructing and modifying lists

New lists may be formed from existing objects by the function list(). An assignment of the form

> Lst <- list(name_1=object_1, ..., name_m=object_m)

This sets up a list Lst of m components using object 1, . . . , object m for the components and giving them names as specified by the argument names, (which can be freely chosen). If these names are omitted, the components are numbered only. The components used to form the list are copied when forming the new list, and the originals are not affected.

Lists, like any subscripted object, can be extended by specifying additional components. For example

Lst[5] <- list(matrix=Mat)

Concatenating lists

When the concatenation function c() is given list arguments, the result is an object of mode list also, whose components are those of the argument lists joined together in sequence.

> list.ABC <- c(list.A, list.B, list.C)

Recall that with vector objects as arguments the concatenation function similarly joined together all arguments into a single vector structure. In this case, all other attributes, such as dim attributes, are discarded.

attach( ) and detach( )

The $ notation, such as accountants$home, for list components, is not always very convenient. A useful facility would be somehow to make the list or data frame components temporarily visible as variables under their component name, without the need to quote the list name explicitly each time.

The attach( ) function takes a 'database' such as a list or data frame as its argument. Let's say there are three variables in a sample data frame that you are going to work with. Let's say they are used to refer to types of lentils. Here is what we have so far: lentils$w, lentils$v, and lentils$u. Now, consider the following attach( ) statement:

> attach(lentils)

This statement would put the data frame at the position of the search path if only the variables w, v, or u were not found at position 1. The variables w, v, or u are now available from the data frame as variables in their right. However, if the expression used would look like the following:

> u <- v+w

This time it is not used as a replacement of the data frame's component that is designated as u. Note that no permanent changes were made to the data frame since the component u is masked using another variable (this one is in the working directory). Using the $ notation is the easiest way to do for the data frame to be changed permanently.

> lentils$u <- v+w

You won't be able to view the new value of the u component unless you will detach and attach the data frame again.

The function

> detach()

is to be used to detach the data frame

Any entity that is presently at position 2 will be detached from the search path with the use of the detach function. You will not be able to view the w, v, and u variables unless they will be included in the lentils$u list notation and so forth. For entities that are positioned on the search path at more than 2, it is ideal to use their number when detaching. It is safer to use a name when detaching like detach("lentils") or detach(lentils).

Attaching arbitrary lists

An example of a generic function is attach( ). It is used to attach directories and data frames to be attached to a search path. You can use it to attach other object classes. In the same way, you can also attach any "list" mode objects. The following is an example:

> attach(any.old.list)

Now, you can use the "detach( )" function to reverse the attachment made by the attach( ) generic function. You can use the detach( ) function for anything that has been attached by attach( ). The preferred method is to detach by name however you may also detach using the position number.

Search Path Management

In order to manage the search path in Java, you can use the search( ) function. You can keep track of packages, lists, and data frames using this function. It basically shows the current search path, and you can also use it to check for data frames that have been attached and also detached to the current search path.

search shows the current search path, and so is a very useful way to keep track of which data frames and lists (and packages) have been attached and detached.

The following is a sample syntax of this function:

```
> search( )

[1] ".GlobalEnv"      "Autoloads"    "package:base"
```

In this example .GlobalEnv serves as the workspace.

Here is a sample code that shows the syntax of the detach( ) function. In this sample, the data frame/object "lentils" is detached.

```
detach("lentils")

search( )

[1] ".GlobalEnv"      "Autoloads"    "package:base"
```

Recursive Numerical Integration

Functions may be recursive, and may themselves define functions within themselves. Note, however, that such functions, or indeed variables, are not inherited by called functions in higher evaluation frames as they would be if they were on the search path.

The example below shows a naive way of performing one-dimensional numerical integration. The integrand is evaluated at the end points of the range and in the middle. If the one-panel trapezium rule answer is close enough to the two panel, then the latter is returned as the value. Otherwise, the same process is recursively applied to each panel. The result is an adaptive integration process that concentrates function evaluations in regions where the integrand is farthest from linear. There is, however, a heavy overhead, and the function is only competitive with other algorithms when the integrand is both smooth and very difficult to evaluate.

Example:

```r
area <- function(f, a, b, eps = 1.0e-06, lim = 10) {

fun1 <- function(f, a, b, fa, fb, a0, eps, lim, fun) { ##
function 'fun1' is only visible inside 'area'

d <- (a + b)/2 h <- (b - a)/4 fd <- f(d)

a1 <- h * (fa + fd)

a2 <- h * (fd + fb)

if(abs(a0 - a1 - a2) < eps || lim == 0) return(a1 + a2)

else {

return(fun(f, a, d, fa, fd, a1, eps, lim - 1, fun) + fun(f, d, b,
fd, fb, a2, eps, lim - 1, fun))

}

}

fa <- f(a) fb <- f(b)

a0 <- ((fa + fb) * (b - a))/2

fun1(f, a, b, fa, fb, a0, eps, lim, fun1)

}
```

CHAPTER 8

CLASSES, OBJECTS, AND OTHER OOP CONCEPTS REVISITED

Java and the OOP Rationale

In an earlier chapter of this book, we introduced you to some of the basic concepts of Object Oriented Programming. You learned concepts like objects, classes, inheritances, packages, and interfaces.

The main idea and rationale for object oriented programming have some parallels with the way we assemble desktop computers nowadays. You can say that assembling a desktop computer is relatively easy with the abundance of compatible pieces of hardware today.

You can go to a computer hardware store, buy a motherboard, processor, RAM, hard drive, power supply, casing

You don't have to worry about how many cores the processor has (some have only 1 core while others may have 6 or more). You don't have to worry if the motherboard has four or even six layers. Your hard drive 4 or six plates or maybe it can be a solid state drive.

All you need to do is to make sure that the parts are supported by the motherboard. If that requirement is satisfied, all you need to do is to put everything together. You don't have to worry if your computer parts were made in Taiwan, China, Korea, or anywhere else. Parts can be ported and reused in other computer systems.

The same idea of portability and reusability also exists in our everyday lives. You can replace your light bulb with a newer and more technologically advanced model. Most of the technical roadblocks have been dealt with.

Dealing with hardware in this manner is pretty easy. Now, the question is if you can do that with software. Can you pick-up pieces of code that worked in the past and then assemble them to create a totally new program? The answer is a staggering no. Given all the technological advancements that we have today, we still haven't standardized our software. Ironic isn't it?

The Difficulty with Software

Now, if you're wondering what happened, here it is. Mankind has actually written an astounding amount of software. We have literally written tons of code which includes subroutines, functions, and entire programs and software systems in the past decade. The only problem is that none of them is designed to inter-cooperate from one system or methodological approach to the next. Somebody wrote one operating system, and another guy wrote another, and you will need another software system to act as a go between just to make these two operating systems "talk" to each other.

In other words, for each new software system we make, we have to reinvent the proverbial wheel time and again. It's literally just like starting again from scratch each and every time. Logically, you would ask why do we need to reinvent the wheel if the wheel already works, right?

That is the issue with procedural oriented languages. Examples of such programming languages include Pascal, Cobol, Fortran, and C. Here are the two biggest drawbacks from languages of this type:

- **Their functions are not designed to be complete encapsulated and stand alone**: this means they are not designed to be a self-contained unit. For instance, the functions in these programming languages can reference variables global – these are variables that are declared in the main program body making them accessible to all parts of the program. You can't take these functions and port them to another program since the global variables they reference is most likely absent in the new program being written.
- **They are not suitable for high-level abstraction**: note that a lot of these programs make use of low-level constructs which are primarily used for low-level abstraction. The usual approach with these programming languages is that they focus on the machine – how to make a computer do something rather than how these functions can help solve the issues of a user. These languages deal with the minute details, which is already beyond the scope of high-level abstraction, which is the more common approach that we see today. In

low-level abstraction, data structures and algorithms are taken separately whereas these are taken as a whole in high-level abstraction.

It should be noted that some lower level languages such as C have already incorporated a certain degree of object oriented programming with the incorporation of dynamic data structures. Nevertheless, the main focus for these languages is still on how to make a machine operate, which makes them useful for the functions of new hardware and in the programming of operating systems.

How Object Oriented Programming Languages Differ

Object oriented programming languages like Java takes the focus away from how a computer or a piece of hardware works. It focuses on how to solve a user's problem rather than concerning oneself with how to make a computer function and then try to use that to solve the problem.

Java and other similar high-level programming languages allow higher levels of abstraction. That means the programmer doesn't really have to figure out how a machine does something. It has already been pre-programmed, and you no longer need to focus on that.

Java allows you to focus on the problem and use objects to represent elements a variety of entities that can help solve a problem. But that higher level of abstraction isn't the only advantage of OOP.

As stated elsewhere, the basic unit in Java as well as in other object oriented programming languages is the class. A class encapsulates both the dynamic operations and the data structures to be used in the program.

The idea behind OOP is to make software behave in a similar way to hardware – that is to treat each construct as a type of object ergo the object construct in Java and in other programming languages. In the real world, you can find objects of the same class or type. For instance, there are hundreds of brands and classes of bicycles out there. They may be designed differently, but they still share the same fundamental features. These bicycles still make use of the same fundamental design or blueprint.

And that is basically what a class is – it is the blueprint that all objects follow when they are designed. As stated earlier, Java will consist of a group of objects that are well encapsulated (i.e. they can stand alone) that interact with one another.

Let's say you want to write a bicycle race program. That in itself is a very difficult process if you think about it in low-level terms. However, you can design the program model already in Java by considering the different objects that will be involved in the actual game.

You can already envision the actual objects that you want to see in your race program, which may include the following:

- Rider
- Bicycle
- Race track
- Audience
- Road conditions

You can then model how each of these objects interacts with one another and what messages will be relayed from one element to the other. You can already deduce the information that will be passed along each object and which objects will require certain bits of communication from specific objects in order to determine the winner of the race.

Another important thing that you should notice is the fact that certain objects (and usually all of them) in a Java program can be used by or ported to a different program. For instance, if you are writing another program that also needs an Audience object and Road Conditions object then you can take these objects without any need to modify them and use them in the new program.

Given all that, we can, therefore, outline some of the benefits of object oriented programming in Java. They include the following:

- It makes software design easier.
- You can focus on the problem and the user's needs.
- Maintenance is made easier since you can already get a general view of the entire system or program. This allows you to identify trouble points much faster.
- Software is made reusable and more portable. If you need components or objects in a new program that you already wrote in a previous program, you don't need to rewrite the same object. You can just get the one from the old program and include it in the new one.

Instances and Classes Revisited

As stated earlier, a class in Java is the blueprint that is used to create objects. It defines the attributes of an object as well as the way an object should behave. Some would use the terms template or prototype to describe what a class is. The attributes of a class are static, which means that they don't change while the behaviors are always referred to as being dynamic, which means they are changeable.

Now, we have mentioned in an earlier chapter of this book that another term for an object in Java is "instance." Sometimes these two terms are used interchangeably, but they actually have a subtle difference. For example, let's say we defined a class called Employee. As stated earlier, we can create different objects using this particular class.

Let's say a manager needs to include information for different employees he is considering for promotion. As the programmer, you will make use of the Employee class and define Gina, Jake, and Mark as the different objects of that class. Mark, Jake, and Gina are all Instances of the Employee class. The term object can be used to refer to these instances, and at times it is also used to refer to the Class itself.

Visualizing Classes

To help you understand the concepts of Class, Objects, and Instances, it will be beneficial to imagine them as a kind of compartment with three boxes in it.

Let's go back to the bicycle race program that we mentioned earlier. Let's try to define the Bicycle class visually. It would look something like this:

Bicycle

xLocation yLocation Speed
Stop( ) Moving ( ) Position( ) Accelerate( )

In this example right here we are using what is called the UML class and instance diagrams. UML stands for Unified Modeling Language. As you can see, the diagram above is divided into three different parts or layers. The three compartments illustrated above are the following:

1. Identifier –The top layer of the diagram above is for the identifier or name. This top layer is the name you give to a class. The name should specifically identify and also describe the type of object as seen or experienced by the user. In simple terms, the name or identifier should identify the class.

2. Variables – The second layer of the UML diagram above is for the variables or what has been described as the static attributes of the class that is being defined. This section of the three compartment box is also called the field, state, or attribute. This is actually the area where the data structures are included or contained.

3. Methods – The bottom layer of this diagram contains the methods or the dynamic behaviors of the class. This part tells us about the behavior, the operation, or the program functions that can be performed by the class.

Quick Review: A class is a software entity or construct that is defined by the Java programmer. It is self-contained, which means it does not call out to any global variable or data structure. That means all the data structures it needs are defined within the body of the class.

Classes in Java are reusable software. Classes are also designed to mimic real world things. Note however that classes are not stand alone programs. They do not have the main( ) method as you would define a stand-alone Java program that you can compile and run.

A class is supposed to be a building block. As it is, it is a construct that can be used in the current program and it can also be used in other programs as well. A class has three compartments, which are the following: name, variables, and methods.

Defining a Class in Java

We have touched on the following a little bit in the previous chapters. You need to define a class in order to create one or use one in a Java program. Here is the syntax for a class definition:

[AccessControlModifier] class ClassName {
  // Class body contains members (variables and methods)
  ...
}

To declare or define a class in Java you need to use the keyword or reserved word "class." You can find that highlighted in red in the syntax above. You don't need to highlight it when you write your code – in case you use a text editor or an IDE to write your code. It is just highlighted here so you can spot it easily.

The **[AccessControlModifier]** which comes before the reserved word/keyword can either be "private" or "public." We'll go over that in detail below.

What are Access Control Modifiers?

We already mentioned that access control modifiers can either be public or private. Simply put, you will use it to control the visibility of a member variable or of the class itself. You have been introduced to two access control modifiers, namely:

1. Public – this means the class, method, or variable being declared is accessible to all of the other objects that you declare or create in your program/system.
2. Private – this means that the method or variable being declared will only be made available within the body of the class (i.e. not accessible to outside objects).

Note that there are other access control modifiers other than these two.

ClassName and Naming Conventions

The ClassName is user defined, and the usual naming conventions require programmers to use noun phrases or just nouns. That means you can name a class using several words if you wish. When using multiple words, use camel case. Always use a singular noun for the class name – no plurals as much as possible.

Creating an Instance

The next step after defining a class, you need to create the instances of the class that you have defined. So let's say we have defined the Employee class and we want to create 3 different instances of that class namely Jeff, Joan, and Jeremy. Here are the steps:

1. The first step is to use the name of the name the class to declare the instances that we want to make. So, in this example of ours, we will use the following syntax:

    Employee Jeff, Joan, Jeremy;

2. The next step is to initialize the instances. We will use the "new" operator to perform that action, like so:

    jeff = new Employee( );
    joan = new Employee( );
    jeremy = new Employee( );

alternatively, you can also do these two actions in one line, like so:

Employee Jeff = Employee( );

Note that if you only declare an instance, perhaps you forgot to construct it as you write your code, that instance will hold the value which is called *null*.

Invoking a Method

To invoke a method, you need to identify the instance by using the dot operator. So let's say you want to invoke the getHoursWorked( ) method given the employee instances that we created earlier; you will use the following line:

jeff. getHoursWorked( )

Note that calling the getHoursworked( ) method and not identifying the instance you want to include will yield nothing since we have already created more than one instance of the class Employee. Note that each instance should have its own value for hours worked.

The same is true when you work with member variables. Methods and variables that belong to a class are called member methods and member variables.

So let's say you have a variable in the class that is called aHourlyRate, you will use the dot operator in much the same way, like so:

jeff.aHourlyRate

Auto Boxing

This method of invoking or calling a method using a dot operator is the way to do it before Java 5. That is until the concept of auto boxing was introduced. Before auto boxing was introduced, if you want to call a method with associated primitive data types then you have to use a dot operator. With auto boxing, you no longer need to. Java will automatically box that primitive data variable to an object.

For example, say we want to invoke or call method with an integer value, the usual way to do it was to do the following:

```
Integer mySampleInteger = new Integer(50);
int myInt1 = mySampleInteger.intValue( );
```

With auto boxing, your code will be shortened. The above code will then look like this:

```
Integer mySampleInteger = new Integer(50);
    int myInt1 = mySampleInteger;
```

This way with auto boxing Java will just extract the value of the int from the object that you specified, which is mySampleInteger. It will do that automatically. The system will then assign the extracted value to myInt1. That's how easy it is with Java 5 and newer. Note that if you are still using an older version, then you can't do auto boxing. Check which one you are using.

Auto boxing also works with creating new versions of an object. If a new version of an object has a primitive data type associated with it, you no longer have to do it manually. Going back to the same example above, here is how you do it in the older versions of Java:

```
int myInt1 = 50;
Integer mySampleInteger2 = new Integer(myInt1);
```

Auto boxing simplifies that too. Here's how it is done with auto boxing:

```
int myInt1 = 50;
Integer mySampleInteger2 = myInt1;
```

Just remember that with auto boxing you don't have to do things manually. Java will automatically box any primitive data type inside the new object version. Note however that this system is not fool proof. If a variable references an object (i.e. the type of the variable is an object), then that means it can also point to nothing or null.

You will get an error (i.e. NullPointerException) when you try to compile and then run a code where you convert null to a primitive data type or value. Here is an example of code that will produce that error. You can try to compile and run that if you want just to produce the said error:

```
Integer myErroneousInteger = null;
int myInt1 = myErroneousInteger;
```

Note that the code above may compile with no problems. But when it is executed it will result in the NullPointerException error. It is impossible to unbox an integer variable (according to the example above) pointing to null – simply put, it points to nothing, and you can't convert an object that is pointing to nothing, logically speaking.

More on Member Variables

Variables in Java have a type and an identifier. Their function is to hold a value given its type. Variable names also follow certain conventions. Their names should be nouns or noun phrases (i.e. more than one word). The first word should be in lower case. The rest of the words will be in camel case. Consider the following examples

- aMotorCycle
- topSpeed

- timeLimit
- xGridNumber

Here is the syntax for declaring a variable in a Java:

```
[AccessControlModifier] type variableName [= initialValue];

[AccessControlModifier] type variableName-1 [= initialValue-1] [, type variableName-2 [= initialValue-2]] ... ;
```

As it was explained earlier in this book, variables are memory allocations that hold a data value. Every data value has a specific type. The data types in Java can be categorized into two types:

1. Primitive data types
2. Object references

We have already covered the data types in Chapter 5 of this book. You can go back to that chapter in case you need to refresh your memory.

Method Naming Conventions

We shall revisit the naming conventions in Java since you will be using member methods. Methods in Java programming perform operations, they also receive any argument provided by a caller, and it can also return a result of an operation to a caller. Here's the syntax for declaring a method:
[Access Control Modifier] Return Type methodName ([set of parameters]) {
  // body of the method
   ......
}
Here are a few rules to remember when you make the names for the methods that you will write. Method names are always verbs or more specifically verb phrases

(which means you can use multiple words to name them). The first word of the method name should all be in lower case letters while the rest of the words should follow a camel case format. Here is an example:

writeMethodNamesThisWay( )

Now, you should remember that verbs are used for method names, and they indicate an action while nouns are used for variable names, and they denote a certain attribute.

Following the syntax for declaring a method and following the name conventions for this Java construct, here's a sample code that can be used to compute the area of a circle.

```java
public double computeCircleArea() {
return radius * radius * Math.PI;
}
```

Using Constructors in Your Code

We have already described constructors in Chapter 10 of this book. We'll just go over some additional details as they relate to object oriented programming. As stated earlier, a constructor will look like a method, and you can certainly think of it and treat it like a special kind of method in Java programming.

However, a constructor will still be different from a method in several ways. The name of a constructor will be the same as the class name. Use the keyword or operator "new" to create a new instance of the constructor and also to initialize it. Here's an example using the class "Employee" and a variety of ways to initialize it in your code:

```
Employee payrate1 = new Employee( );
Employee payrate2 = new Employee(2.0);
Employee payrate3 = new Employee(3.0, "regular");
```

A constructor will also implicitly return void – that simply means it doesn't have a return type. You can't put a return statement inside the body of a constructor since it will be flagged by compilers as an error. The only way you can invoke a constructor is via the use of the "new" statement. We have already given you several ways how you can invoke constructors in the samples above.

One final difference is that constructors can't be inherited. Let's go back to the examples provided above – the first line includes "Employee( );" – that is called a default constructor. As you can see, it has no parameters whatsoever. The job of a default constructor is to simply initialize the member variables to a specific default value. In the example above, the member variable payrate1 was initialized to its default pay rate and employee status.

Can constructors be overloaded too? Yes, they can. Constructors behave like methods too so that means you can overload a constructor just the same way you overload a method. Here are a few examples on how you can overload a constructor. We use the Employee class and overload it using different parameters.

```
Employee( )
Employee(int r)
Employee(int r, String b)
```

CHAPTER 9

FURTHER OOP CONCEPTS

In the previous chapter, we mentioned two types of access control modifiers, public and private. In this chapter, we will introduce you to two more keywords that are also used as access control modifiers. They will be discussed in the next section which covers information hiding and encapsulation.

Information Hiding and Encapsulation Compared

Information hiding is one of the key features of the Java programming language and object oriented programming. You have already been introduced to this concept in part we covered concepts on data abstraction. Simply put, an object in Java will usually hide how it implements its own functionality.

Now, in order to do that, you will have to make use of access control modifiers. Here are four of them:
- Public
- Private
- Protected
- Default

You are already familiar with the first two – public and private. When the variable is declared to be public then it can be anywhere in the program you are writing. In contrast when it is private then it can't be seen or accessed anywhere else but in the body of the class where it has been instantiated.

Let's move on to the other two access control modifiers. The next one on the list is called "protected" – which is useful in case you want to create libs. When a variable is protected, it means that it can only be seen within the package where this Java construct has been instantiated – note that this also includes all the subclasses.

The "default" access control modifier, on the other hand, is used by the variable when the other three aren't specified. In this mode, a variable can be accessed within package or class where it has been instantiated by the programmer. However, do take note that the variable is only accessible within the main body of the class and it is not available within its subclasses.

Note that you can also create an object within a method and the usual rules apply – the object or variable can only be accessed within the body of the method where it has been created. Here's another important point that you should remember about variables that you create within a method – it can only specify one keyword for it: final. You will not be allowed to create a default, protected, public, or even a private variable within the method body. And that is basically how information is hidden in your code, which, if you observe, facilitates data abstraction and encapsulation.

Encapsulation? Information Hiding? What's the Difference? It would appear at first glance that encapsulation and data or information hiding may look the same, but there is indeed a subtle difference between these two terms. Now, Nat Pryce and Steve Freeman has made quite an accurate distinction between these two although you may read from other authors who use these terms interchangeably.

We'll use Freeman and Pryce's descriptions here to draw the difference between these two concepts in Java programming. Let's begin with information hiding since that is where we left off. You can already judge what "information hiding" means. It simply means information is concealed. The actual functions and procedures performed by the program are concealed.

But, for what purpose? Why are the inner workings kept hidden from the programmer? The lower level details are ignored so that you, the programmer, can focus on much more important things. That is also why data is abstracted in Java. You can create classes, objects, and other elements of your program; you can even import objects from one program to another without worrying about the details on how that object does what it does.

It's like driving a car. All you need to know is that when you insert your key into the keyhole and start the car, it will start. You don't have to worry about what makes it start, how the wires are connected underneath there, where the gas goes, how the engine burns the gas, etc. All you need to worry about is starting the car and driving safely.

Encapsulation, on the other hand, allows the user to control the amount of change in an object can affect the other parts of class. The term "encapsulate" means to enclose everything in a singular cell. That means that given the way the Java programming system is designed, there will be no expected dependency from one independent cell to another. Remember that objects within the Java programming environment are meant to be stand alone, and there are no global variables to reference.

Inheritances and Subclasses in Java Programming

Earlier we mentioned classes have subclasses. We'll look into that in this section. We have already indicated in this book that objects in Java may have certain traits of characteristics common to a group especially if they are related.

For example, let's say we have the following classes:
- Tricycle
- RoadBike
- TandemBike
- BmxBike
- MountainBike

They will all share the same qualities and functionalities such as pedal cadence, speed, number of passengers, etc. Obviously, each of these objects is a type of bicycle. Now, inherently, these classes also have characteristics that are unique to them. For instance, a Tricycle will have one wheel in front, and two wheels at the back and its passenger is usually a child. A MountainBike, on the other hand, will have only one passenger, and it will usually have multiple gears. A BmxBike is smaller, single passenger, but is a better fit for performing tricks or for rough terrain such as in extreme sports.

In Java, as well as in other object oriented programming languages, classes are allowed to "inherit" certain characteristics from other classes. In the example above, you can create a super class called Bicycle which will contain all the characteristics that all these other classes share.

The Bicycle class will become the super class and Tricycle, RoadBike, TandemBike, BmxBike, and MountainBike will become the subclasses. Do take note that Java a subclass or a class can have only one super class. There is no limit for super classes – they can have as many subclasses as needed.

To create a subclass, you will need to use the reserved word or keyword "extends." Here is the syntax for creating the BmxBike subclass:

```
class BmxBike extends Bicycle {
//this is where the methods and other fields go
}
```

In this example, the BmxBike subclass will now get all the same fields and methods that are already found in the Bicycle super class. You can then add the methods and fields that make the BmxBike subclass unique.

Conclusion

Thank you again for taking the time out of your schedule to download JAVA Programming: Intermediate Concepts for the Fundamentals of Object Oriented Programming! Keep an eye out for the final book in the series.

If you have enjoyed this book as much as I have enjoyed writing it, I ask that you please take the time to leave me a review on Amazon. I appreciate your positive feedback!